FLOS MALVAE

FLOS MALVAE

BY

A. B. RAMSAY

MASTER OF MAGDALENE COLLEGE
CAMBRIDGE

AUTHOR OF *INTER LILIA*
ROS ROSARUM AND
FRONDES SALICIS

CAMBRIDGE

AT THE UNIVERSITY PRESS

1946

CAMBRIDGE
UNIVERSITY PRESS

University Printing House, Cambridge CB2 8BS, United Kingdom

Cambridge University Press is part of the University of Cambridge.

It furthers the University's mission by disseminating knowledge in the pursuit of education, learning and research at the highest international levels of excellence.

www.cambridge.org
Information on this title: www.cambridge.org/9781316601716

© Cambridge University Press 1946

First published 1946
First paperback edition 2015

A catalogue record for this publication is available from the British Library

ISBN 978-1-316-60171-6 Paperback

Stand the mallows, tall and flowering,
  Proudly towering over all;
Lowly shall they stoop, and slowly
  Fade and fall.

Man, the strong and great and clever,
  Builds an everlasting state;
Dying, yet he dies defying
  Time and Fate.

Droop autumnal flowers and vernal;
  Stand eternal walls and towers,
Rhyming with the years, and chiming
  Golden hours.

Faith is thronèd o'er the portal;
  Love immortal guards the door,
Keeping watch with eyes unsleeping
  Evermore.

PROPTER FRATRES MEOS

When to the clash of battle
    The need of England calls,
Magdalene our lovely Lady,
    Peace be within thy walls.

May hearts be slow to anger,
    And voices swift to bless,
And in thy house of honour
    Be nought but gentleness.

Thy sons, in fire and fury,
    In sand and cloud and foam,
With tears of love remember
    What peace was in thy home.

Remembering, and remembered,
    Not doubting that they see
Thy quiet ways untroubled,
    They turn their eyes on thee.

TALLEYRAND

Nulli non homini nullo non tempore Crassus
  mentitur, nec qui decipiatur habet.
En ego dissimilis. Nusquam quia mentior, omnes
  orbis terrarum decipio populos.

THE GOURMET

Quae res Aemilio multos curaverat annos
  hoc narratur anus non sine teste loqui:
'Non prodesse quod est, et non quod potat obesse
  quod solet Aemilio, me tenet attonitam.'

THE MASTER

Aedibus inspectis annosi Galla Magistri
  'Numquis in hac', inquit, 'vivere tabe potest?'
'Si fas vera loqui', socius respondit amice,
  'anxietas animi non ea nostra fuit.'

TO G.W.H.

Non est ut dubitem viam vorare,
iucundissime, te vocante, Tuppi.
Io Hymen Hymenaee concinemus
atque Antoniolo meo tuoque
ut sint omnia fausta comprecantes
non unum calicem hauriemus ambo.
O me caelicolis parem futurum,
O dulcem mihi commorationem.

TO MR DEAS

Non satis est alias forma superare puellas;
una—nec immerito—vincit Iona Deas.

CONSISTENCY

Choerogenes, qui sus animo est et nomine, iactat
'En, mihi quam constans sum similisque mei.'
Quam bene se iactet, Mummi, fateare necesse est,
et sibi quam constans sit, similisque sui.

DOLCE FAR NIENTE

Nil agere est, inquam, tum dulce in sole vacanti
  Omnia cum pro me naviter alter agit.

    Doing nothing's pleasant,
      Lying in the sun,
    If there's someone present
      Who sees that things are done.

JURA

I

Cura non semper sequitur nocentem
Aut ratem scandit rapidumque currum;
Nuper immunis patria relicta
    Me quoque fugi,
Iule, te certo duce, te perito
Sospes auriga. Fluvio lacuque et
Monte frondoso viridique saltu
    Lumina pavi
Liber et laetus. Quibus excitata
Gaudiis inter trepidos tumultus,
Quae manet coram penitusque nostros
    Sentit amores,
Musa quodcunque hoc tibi, qualecunque est,
Versuum profert animique grates,
Prae tuo quam sit leve, quam sit impar,
    Conscia donum.

JURA

II

Pastus aerumnas animique lassus
Non eget taetris medici venenis
Aut Atlanteos reparante soles,
    Fusce, Liburna,
Si lacus alti virides Iurae
Visit et saltus placidos et amnes
Rupe pendentes et imaginosa
    Fontibus antra.
Namque ibi fido comiti ducique
Dum vehor iunctus taciteque mecum
Versibus ludo, gravis otiantem
    Cura refugit,
Caerulo qualis cooperta amictu
Adsidet lectis hominum, aut aperta
Luce furtivis operosiores
    Vocibus ambit.
Pone me parvae super urbe Balmae,
Qua per occultos properat recessus
Silia, et splendent cumulata vivo
    Moenia saxo;
Pone qua circa est oculos et aures
Omne quod captat: procul exsulanti
Dulce ridebit numerosa Clio,
    Dulce loquetur.

TEA

Bacchicum iactant alii liquorem;
Dona Pomonae Cererisque ducunt;
Zinziver zytho vel acerba miscent
    Hordea lymphis.
Omnibus dictis tamen atque factis,
Te, latex Serum, potiore dignor
Laude; te prima prece, te suprema
    Laetus adoro.

A DOUBTFUL QUANTITY

APOPHORETON

Latin Dictionary:

Tamesis an Tamesis, dubitat si forte poeta,
    pagina praesentem nostra ministrat opem.

G.B.F.
T.L.S

TO G.B.F. AND T.L.S.

Tamesis, an Tamesis? Dubitant fugiuntque poetae.
    Discipulos produnt decipiuntque libri.
O fortunatos iuvenes, sua si bona norint.
    Rebus in incertis, ecce, Magister adest.

TO C.M.W.

Mense taces toto, nec sum, quae vina bibamus,
  quove die venias, certior, inve quotum.
Praetereunt anni; furtim venit aegra senectus;
  cras morimur; prudens, Deipnosophista, veni.

TO G.S.R.K.C.

Si tam multa places et tam festiva loquendo,
  semper ego auditor. Parcere parce loqui.
Cum Iove cenabo quoties cenabis apud me;
  ambrosia pascar, vinaque nectar erunt.

TO S.B.

AUGUST 3

Hunc ego cum sociis celebro mensemque diemque
  quo tu natus eras quoque ego natus eram.
Cancellarius es. 'Bene te Fortuna secundet'
  dicimus, et 'Bis sex funde, puer, cyathos.'

THE TWIG

Quam puer est plantae similis. Si neglegis, Acci,
  squalet, et in toto turpiter errat agro.
Si regis, incomptos cernis discedere mores;
  pullulat, et pulchre floret, et ornat humum.

THE SUN

Sol ubi lascivus puerorum provocat iras,
    et nitidum spisso condit in imbre caput,
Furius impatiens 'O detestabile caelum'
    clamat, et 'O pestes', et pede tundit humum.
Non ego; sed mecum sedeo subductus in umbram,
    et videor picto totus inesse libro.
Tum Sol festivus vano certamine cedit;
    ora aperit ridens perfruiturque ioco.

THE PLACE FOR SONG

Frigida per virides currunt ubi flumina campos,
    et vitreae molli voce loquuntur aquae,
undique qua monstrat mixtos Natura colores,
    et variat vento populus alba comas,
illic Pierii gaudent errare poetae,
    et facilis gratum Musa coronat opus.

THE FOUR SEASONS

Vere novo decorant nascentia germina dumos;
    purpureis aestas floribus opplet humum;
aureus ostendit flavas auctumnus aristas;
    cincta pruinoso rore coruscat hiems.
Omnis dividitur partes in quattuor annus,
    quae me delectant ordine quaeque suo.

VERSES IN WINTER

Tempore quo fluvium pinnis astringit hirundo,
  et cytisos circum rara susurrat apis,
qua salices pendent, et floret aquatica lotus,
  limpida qua molli murmurat unda sono,
tum numeri veniunt, tum mente et corpore liber
  Pieridum perago dulce libenter opus.
Nunc premimus duri subsellia dura magistri,
  nunc hebetant nostras frigora saeva manus,
nunc animus nobis toto cum corpore torpet,
  et solitam frigens Musa negavit opem.
Hos tamen extuderim quo vix ego numine versus,
  si possum vobis dicere, dispeream.

THE RIGHT MATERIAL

Iam nunc disce, puer, lingua cantare Latina;
  materiam quali sis numerosus habes.
Tam bene non alias aptantur carmina verbis;
  tam bene tornantur non aliunde modi.
Nimirum quibus est acies acerrima caelis
  artifices gaudent, et rude fulget opus.
Linea nulla placet, calamo nisi ducis acuto;
  nec secat aequales serra retusa trabes.
Tum lyra (nec sine teste loquor) fit grata canenti,
  non laxas digiti cum tetigere fides.
Ausonii manibus sumas, puer, arma poetae;
  sumpta suas artes saepius arma docent.

A GREAT DISCOVERY

Decipimur rerum specie puerilibus annis;
  nescio qui teneris visibus error obest.
Saepe puer tacitus mecum ridere solebam
  quae mihi praesedit, Flacce, magistra cohors.
Saepe puer dixi 'Tam rara animalia nusquam
  vidimus aut tali corpora facta modo.'
In caecis homines tenebris quam saepe vagantur,
  nec cernunt ipsos quod iacet ante pedes.
Nunc mihi vera patent. Res est contraria tota;
  ipse animal rarum est ridiculumque puer.
Cum pueros doceo, risus vix abdere possum,
  nec magis oblectant pulpita plena ioco.

MRS BUSYBODY

Ne supra crepidam cupiat discedere sutor;
  ne properent multi ius vitiare coci.
Non bene quae vetita est arcam, Pandora, resignas;
  flammantes, Phaethon, non bene iungis equos.
En, Polypragmosyne quam multa negotia curat;
  en, agilis tota miscet in urbe manus.
Circumspectatrix anus est; adsistit; inaudit;
  civibus invitis improba praebet opem.
Nullas in latebras nonvult intrudere nasum;
  quaslibet in lances inserit articulos.
Dirige tu tua vela, tuum propelle phasellum;
  quidquid agunt alii, res age, Marce, tuas.
Nauta soporatum quam paene exstinxit Vlixen
  cum rabidos arto solvit ab utre notos.
Felis erat. Voluit rerum cognoscere causas.
  Investigantem perdidit illa sitis.

GRAMMAR

Nuper oberrabam nemoris deiectus in umbra,
   dum miser Orbilium Grammaticenque queror.
Grammatice venit vestes induta decoras;
   et, memini, certos movit ab arte pedes.
Vidit et arrisit laeto pulcherrima voltu,
   et mihi 'Quid ploras,' dixit, 'inepte puer?'
Vt didicit causam, molli me murmure mulcens
   alloquitur: 'Culpa falleris ipse tua.
'Nonne vides quam sim facilis iucundaque dictu?
   'Desipiunt pueri me nisi prorsus amant.'
Nec mora; dinumerat casus, et tempora cantat;
   aptamusque chorum, conserimusque manus.
Nomina subsiliunt; circum pronomina saltant,
   verbaque per varios distribuenda modos.
Mensa vocat *mensam*; resonant *mordere, momordi*;
   sunt ioca, sunt risus qua fuit ante labor.

OUT OF THE BLUE

Nuper me, Licini, poteras prosternere pluma;
   vix fuit attonitis auribus ulla fides.
Namque sedebamus iussi versare Maronem,
   cum subito Orbilius dixit 'Abite foras.'
Dixit 'Abite foras; prompti docilesque fuistis;
   'otia pro meritis iusta referre placet.'
Nulla mora est; laeti rapimus fustemque pilamque;
   luditur in viridi caespite; prata sonant.
Vndique ridebat totus sine nubibus aether,
   et tepido mollis vere virebat humus.
Sol et gramineus suadebant gaudia campus;
   effluit ex animis neglegiturque Maro.
Nescio an Orbilius (nam sunt et in orbibus orbes)
   cum grege gestierit ludere et ipse suo.

CAVE

Prospice, si salies: vetus est nec inutile dictum:
  nam parat incautis abdita fossa malum.
Saepe inopina, puer, deprendit Poena nocentes;
  et citius solito saepe magister adest.

GLASS HOUSES

Cur similem aurito semper me dicis asello,
  turpior hirsuto Caeciliane capro?
Non illi lapides aliis infligere debent,
  qui fragiles habitant, vitrea tecta, domos.

EL DORADO

Saepe pater dicit 'Si custodiveris asses,
  'nummus erit custos aureus ipse sui.
'Saepe homines periere suis potiora petendo;
  'stultitiae poenam saepe dedere suae.
'Perdidit os catulus maioris imagine captus;
  'pluris erat quoties una duabus avis.'
At pueri dites parvo sunt tempore facti,
  credere si scriptis possumus historiis.
Tardo divitias alii conamine quaerant;
  longa mora est culmen per tot adire gradus.
Inveniam regum gazas aurumque sepultum;
  mox findet spoliis navis onusta fretum.
Tum repetam dulcem patriam carosque penates;
  excipiet tum me non sine laude pater.

HAPPY AND WISE

Astra quot in caelo, quot sunt in cespite flores,
   quot folia in silvis leniter aura movet,
vel quot apud coctam numerabis pruna placentam,
   tot sunt in vita gaudia, Quinte, mea.
Sed praesaga meam retinet prudentia mentem;
   qua bona sunt, aliquid suspicor esse mali.
Exiguam ambrosio reperimus in unguine muscam;
   et solet in molli spina latere rosa.

PHYSICAL TRAINING

Nunc inter populos minor est reverentia mentis;
   quaeritur in salvo corpore prima salus.
Discipulis tendunt nervos torquentque magistri
   articulos. Matres hoc medicique probant.
'Sic eris utilior', dicunt; 'formosior ibis;
   'sic iuvenis patrio nomine dignus eris.'
Ergo imitor saltu ranas agilesque cicadas,
   et supero frictum mobilitate cicer.
Si querimur duros nisus acremque laborem,
   at ferimus firma perpetimurque fide.
Perpetimur taciti: nam fit fuga nulla querendo;
   nulla fuga est, matres si medicique probant.
Si medici matresque iubent, parentque magistri,
   est asini causas quaerere; nulla fuga est.

SEE-SAW

Proposito Varius nunquam persistit eodem;
　　instabili similis mens agitatur aquae.
Nunc hanc in partem, nunc se convertit in illam,
　　et saepe in medio flumine mutat equum.
Vt pueri 'video' clamant 'vidi'-que vicissim,
　　sic levat, alternam sic premit ille trabem.
Ridiculum est animal; visus vertigine turbat;
　　nescit utro iam sit cauda caputve loco.

OBSTINATE

Non argumentis superatur Claudius unquam;
　　tantum proficiens alloquerere domum.
Caucasium citius dictis adamanta movebis,
　　aut precibus cedet natus ad arma chalybs.
Sic immota manet ventorum flamine quercus,
　　sic riget oceani fluctibus icta silex.
'Quod dixi', dicit, 'dixi.' Si mille reclamant,
　　vanum opus est. Clauso Claudius ore silet.

TASTELESS

Est puer Hermogenes: sensu discernere nescit
  quidquid odoriferum est dissimilesve cibos.
Nil sapiunt huius dulcissima fraga palato;
  naribus appositam nescit olere rosam.
Omnia sunt eadem, nec cretae est caseus impar.
  Me miseret pueri. Quam male natus erat.
Hoc unum invideo: sine questu combibit ullo
  castoreos haustus. 'Sunt mihi nectar,' ait.

THE STRAW

Culmus ego a volgo temnor. Tu saepius aequo
  'culmi non facio' dicis, inepte puer.
At superimpositus confregi terga cameli;
  nautaque me captat dum perit inter aquas.
Nec facile est sine me lateres effingere limo,
  nec liquidam e vitreo sugere vase citrum.
Vnde aurae veniant, per me discernitur unum.
  I nunc, tu flocci me fac, inepte puer.

YOREDALE AND JURA

Valle super tota sonitu tonat unda tremendo;
    turbidus admissos urget Iurus equos.
At procul hinc viridi pulcherrima Nais in antro
    continuum liquido stamine texit opus.
Ducitur in longos tractus argenteus imber;
    sic tereti bysso lintea palla cadit.
Ipsa suis manibus vestem Natura creavit;
    ars hominum tantae vincitur arte deae.

JACK OF ALL TRADES

Nunc sequitur magnos parvus Caracalla poetas;
    inter conscriptos nunc sedet ille patres;
Nunc vult orator, nunc mavult esse tragoedus;
    nunc ait 'organicus', nunc 'ego pictor ero.'
Ars hominum est unam servare fideliter artem;
    omnia qui captat, nil, Caracalla, capit.

DILEMMA

Cur me semper habes per tot discrimina rerum
    cornibus impositum, triste Dilemma, tuis?
Quid faciam, incertum est, vel utro me vertere possim;
    haec non sunt illis anteferenda malis.
Illinc Scylla vorax letalia brachia tendit;
    hinc vomit alternas dira Charybdis aquas.
Tartareos ignes inter pelagusque profundum
    perniciem exspecto funereumque diem.

TROY

Grandia qua stabant invictae moenia Troiae
vix effossa solo fragmina pauca manent.
Huc veniunt hilares longinquo ex orbe Britanni;
rident et prandent, dedita turba ioco.
Transiliunt muros pueri mollesque puellae,
Hectora qua raptum fleverat Andromache.

THE DULL DOG

Omnia sunt eadem Bruto; frigusque calorque
sunt eadem; nullos odit amatve cibos.
Non nimium curat, Boreas adspiret an Auster;
aequo animo purum fert pluviumque Iovem.
Non est ver bruma melius, non gratior illi
sol nebulis; vinum nescit aquamne bibat.
Picturasne videt? non haec praeponitur illi;
hoc illi par est carmen idemque sonat.
Fronte sedens 'Servet Regem Deus' audit operta,
di magni, comites indecoratque suos.
Omnia sunt eadem puero; puer omnibus idem est,
omnis iners, omnis lentus et insipiens.

BLACK OR WHITE

Pleraque sunt, Laeli, mediocria iudice volgo;
  'pleraque nec bona sunt nec mala', volgus ait.
Ferreus hanc lancem Critias aut deprimit illam,
  nec medii quicquam ponderis esse sinit.
Aut atrum Critiae quod ubique est esse videtur
  aut album; non est inter utrumque color.
Aut amat aut odit; comitum discrimine certo
  tot capita in partes dividit ille duas.
Laudibus extollit caules, et tubera damnat;
  'nil pipere est melius, nil sale peius', ait.
Sunt in deliciis catuli; fastidia feles
  dira movent; follem spernit, ovatque pila.
Ipse—nec iniustum est—nusquam mediocris habetur;
  sunt quibus est albus, sunt quibus ater homo.

THE HIGH-BROW

Prisce, vides illum iuvenem qui fronte superba
  prominet, et tollit grande supercilium?
Dicitur ingenio nostras transcendere mentes,
  rebus et humanis editiora sequi.
Aegre Vergilium laudat; fastidit Homerum;
  culpat Apelleas obloquiturque manus.
Mys in contemptu est illi; nil Mentora curat;
  illius ante oculos nil sine labe nitet.
Nempe hominum exaudit tristi praeconia risu;
  nostra opera aetheria spectat ab arce Iovis.
Fusa est caesaries, et mollia verba morantur;
  admissa in summas est coma curta genas.
Languidus ingreditur, vel lento corpore pendet;
  in digitis fulget gemma, fluitque toga.
Exteriora oculos fallunt: interprete tali
  quis putet ostendi, Prisce, placere deo?

FOUNDERS' DAY, 1938

I pro me, rosa regii coloris,
hoc electa die meis ab hortis,
verbis Praepositum meis saluta.
I dic 'accipias Magister orat
quem mittit tibi Magdalena florem,
nata et non alio beata rege,
dans aequaliter et petens amorem'.

TO C.M.W.

Bellona magnos dum populos quatit,
dum terret urbes fulmine et excitat
    stridore per noctes acuto
       his meritos meliora cives,
quo more vivas, optime Fontium,
rescribe, vel qua temporibus malis
    sis mente. Me paucas in horas
       munere continuo solutum,
plenus fabarum et spretor inertiae
dilecta binis dum vehor orbibus
    per rura securus meaque
       pace fruor Lalagenque canto,
prostravit ingens machina; sed celer
delapsus alto Mercurius polo,
    tutela sectantum Camenas,
       eripuit trepidantem ab Orco.
Quam paene vidi tecta Proserpinae
Annamque Reginam et Leporem et meos
    tot morte divisos sodales
       Elysiis vacuos in arvis.
Dis redde grates non sine Massico
umore, si me diligis ut prius;
    si forte res angusta vexat,
       funde tamen cyathos Sabini.

RESCRIPT

Me magna torquet cura, quod audio
te, dum per agros carpis iter tuum,
   motore bo praetervolante
     esse rotis prope funeratum.
Quam saepe dixi 'quid iuvat orbibus
vectum duobus currere per vias,
   quem iam senescentem deceret
     sacra domus coluisse tutum?'
Tu semper audax admonitus meos
ventis dedisti, qualiter Icarus
   sprevit retentantem parentem,
     credidit et male cautus alis.
Tollas Sabinum: nos melioribus
exhauriamus Massica poculis,
   laetique fugisti quod Orcum
     non sine dis, Aries, bibamus.

C. M. W.

Your lines with their classic Latinity win;
I have opened a Massic from innermost bin.

A. B. R.

TO G.W.H.

Qui caelum captat, piscatur in aere, Tuppi,
nec fas est hominem divom contingere vitam;
nec iam litoris illa fides est Hesperidum nec
auriferae fulgentis eburnis urbibus orae.
Sed terrestria sunt vicinaque gaudia nobis,
carpere si possis, carptis feliciter uti.
Quid bonus et sapiens? Romae vel rure beatus
scit vitam regere humane, ac mediocriter ampla
sorte frui, sed praecipue cum nota recessit
ad iuga secretosque lacus, et tesqua nemusque
cum sociis, urbana insignis fronte, pererrat,
ditior Arsacidis. Virtus et simplicitas et
gratia prandentem commendant aut ubi cena
digna Mida posita est et non sine consule testa,
seu focus exstruitur lignis et multa recurrunt
temporis anteacti, et dulcem memoramus Etonam,
quid fuerit Lepus, et Damon, quid Toddius olim,
ni potius lentae placuere silentia menti,
quali homines penitus secum sermone fruuntur,
et, cum saepe tacent, vox est tamen inter amicos.
Haec agis, haec tua sunt; et, si mecum facis, hoc est
denique quod curas eliminat ingeniisque
plus nimio duris risum requiemque ministrat,
unde valent. Quid quaeris? ego istinc sanus abivi
mente animoque vigens et corpore, teque magistrum,
te medicum agnosco, te recto more docentem
vivere. Nimirum cives civilia laudant
praemia, ruricolis arrident ruris honores;
urbi tu rus admisces, mus unus uterque.
'Verum et tu sequeris victum, aut ego fallor, eundem;
sunt totidem tua.' Pol, confers acipensere maenam;
ista nec auderem, nec possem acquirere cultu.

Vive, vale; semper qua nunc geris arte geras rem.
In strepitum ac fumum via me ferrata trahebat
haec tibi dictantem, meditor dum plurima mecum et
quam laetus fuerim et te sim visente futurus.

TO C.M.W.

21 MARCH 1941

Septiens denos numerantis annos
da, puer, Fontis, sed et ebrioso
gaudia et risus et amica misce
    vota Falerno.
Saeviant armis populi per orbem;
hanc libet noctem celebrare cenis,
cui diem, vertens in aprica terras,
    Iuppiter aequat.
Vere nascuntur bona; vere natum
prosequor cantu comitem, et beatos
nuntio soles, melioris anni
    callidus auspex.

TO K.W.M.P.

Malo poetae scriptor optimus rerum
das grande—grandes gratias ago—donum;
Sed huic latinos doctus applicas versus.
Ergo poeta quid facit, suis armis
suoque campo victus? aut quid exspectas?
Mittit malum poema, quod potest unum.

LITVS INIQVVM

Adulescentulus quidam subimpudens
a me admonitus quod per inertiam,
cum esset omnium facta probatio,
vixdum in ordinem primum evaserat,
ad secundarios paene relatus, 'O
'domine, facilest', inquit, 'defugere
'Syrtes et Bosporum, sive quis otians
'restat in litore, sive se obruens
'studiosissime semper laboribus
'magna per aequora viam insequitur
'qua explorabitur certa victoria.
'Ego natura sum ferox, et diligo
'rerum angustias; id ago igitur
'ut premam scopulos magno periculo
'quos timent ceteri; nec ego, domine,
'tantis deterreor difficultatibus.
'Mihi proposui primum in ordinem
'ire novissimos inter, et operae
'nec minus aequo nec plus dare nimio,
'victor ut ederer et tenuissimo
'summam discrimine classem attingerem.'

LEADERSHIP

'Este duces hominum', pueros sic instruis omnes.
Omnes si ducunt, Postume, quis sequitur?

If all be true that I do think,
There are five reasons we should drink;
Good wine; a friend; or being dry;
Or lest we should be by and by;
Or any other reason why.

HENRY ALDRICH

Si quodcunque reor, Catulle, verum est,
causae sunt, puto, quinque cur bibamus;
vinum mite; sodalis; aritudo;
aut ne post breve tempus areamus;
aut quaecunque alia est ubique causa.

We think our fathers fools—so wise we grow.
Our wiser sons will doubtless think us so.

Haec magis est sapiens, sed erit sapientior aetas.
    Haec illi similis: stultus utrique parens.

Stultitiae damnamus avos: damnabimur ipsi.
    Sic patre fit docto doctior usque puer.

Turn not aside, O traveller,
  From the long road through the night
To the calm and certain comfort
  Of the flickering warm firelight.

Turn not aside, O wanderer,
  To the sweet fresh meadow-lands,
Where sudden beauty stops the breath
  Like the touch of lovers' hands.

Turn not aside, O seeker,
  From thy search for beauty's light,
Though thy journey lead thee far into
  The dim fear-haunted night.

Turn not aside, O voyager,
  From the green-dark wind-swept wave,
But sail thou on, till fathoms deep
  Thou sleep in thine ocean grave.

Turn not aside, O soldier,
  From the bitter near-lost strife,
For peace incomprehensible
  Awaits thee after life.

JOHN BOUGHEY

τὴν ἐν νυκτὶ κέλευθον, ὁδοιπόρε, τὴν μάλα μακρὴν
μὴ σύ γ᾽ ἀποστρέψῃ, τοῦ πυρὸς ἱέμενος
ἀσπάσιον φαέθοντος ἐπ᾽ ἐσχάρῃ ἠδ᾽ ἀναπαύλης
τῆς ἐχυρῆς. καὶ μὴν μὴ σύ γε πρὸς διερούς
ἡδυπνόους λειμῶνας, ἀλῆτ᾽, ἄπιθ᾽, ὧν χάρις αὐτή
ἐν στόματι ψυχὴν αὐτίχ᾽ ὁρῶντος ἔχει,
ὡς ὅτ᾽ ἐρώντων χεὶρ χειρὸς θίγεν. εἶτα δὲ καὶ σύ,
ὅστις ὁδὸν τείνεις τῆλε πορευόμενος
κάλλεος αὐτὸ τὸ φῶς διζήμενος, ἤν που ἐφεύρῃς,
νύκτα διὰ σκιερὴν ἔνθα πατοῦσι φόβοι,
τοὔργον μὴ προλίπῃς τὸ προκείμενον. εἶτα πλόον σύ,
ναυτίλε, μὴ κάμψῃς ὠκεανὸν περόων
κύματ᾽ ἀν᾽ ἠνεμόεντ᾽ ἰοειδέα, μέχρι περ ἂν δή
βένθεσιν ἐν μεγάλοις τὸν βαθὺν ὕπνον ἕλῃ.
μηδὲ σύ γ᾽, ὦ στρατιῶτα, μεθίστασο τοῦ πολέμοιο,
κἢν ὅσον οὐκ ἐνδοὺς πικρὸν ἄρη συνάγῃς,
κείνη σ᾽ ἐκδέχεται γὰρ ἀπαλλαχθέντα βίοιο
ἡμετέρης μείζων φροντίδος ἡσυχίη.

But in my dream thou cam'st unto me fast,
And unto speech we fell of e'en such things
As please the sons and daughters of great kings;
And I must smile and talk, and talk and smile,
Though I beheld a serpent all the while
Draw nigh to strike thee: then—then thy lips came
Close unto mine; and while with joy and shame
I trembled, in my ears a dreadful cry
Rang, and thou fellest from me suddenly
And lay'st dead at my feet: and then I spake
Unto myself, 'Would God that I could wake',
But woke not, though my dream changed utterly,
Except that thou wert laid stark dead anigh.
Then in this palace were we, and the noise
Of many folk I heard, and a great voice
Rang o'er it ever and again, and said,
Bellerophon who would not love is dead.
But I—I moved not from thee, but I saw
Through the fair windows many people draw
Unto the lists, until withal it seemed
As though I never yet had slept or dreamed,
That all the games went on, where yesterday
Thou like a god amidst of men didst play:
But yet through all the great voice cried and said,
Bellerophon who would not love is dead.
This is the dream—ah, hast thou heard me, then?
Abide no more, I say, among these men:
Think'st thou the world without thy life can thrive,
More than my heart without thy heart can live?

WILLIAM MORRIS

At mihi per somnos properas accedere, et una
colloquio serimus magnorum qualia regum
saepe placet pueris versare et saepe puellis.
Sed risus itero invitos et verba coacta,
serpentem aspectans in te iam invadere et ictum
tollere. Tum vero adrepunt tua proxima labris
labra meis, et laetitia mixtoque pudore
plena tremo, cum terribilis sonat auribus angor;
lapsus es occumbens subito, sensique iacentem
exanimem ante pedes. 'Somnos, deus, excute', dixi
mecum ego; nec vigilo; sed nunc mutata videntur
omnia te praeter porrectum ibi frigore leti.
Rursus in hanc aulam ventum est, strepitusque frequentum
est hominum auditus circum, totasque per aedes
ingens vox etiam atque etiam inclamantis AMORVM
personat INTERIIT CONTEMPTOR BELLEROPHONTES.
Ipsa—nec abstiteram—nitida prodente fenestra
innumeros iuvenes sic ad certamina cerno
confluere ut iam non somnis me visa videre
crediderim, hesternos sed haberi nunc quoque ludos
humano in coetu qua te deus ante ferebas;
et tamen haec inter vox ingens illa remugit
INTERIIT CONTEMPTOR AMORVM BELLEROPHONTES.
Ergo ego quae vidi in somnis tu conscius audis?
Rumpe moras, inquam, neque·enim cunctarier aequum est
hos penes; an censes iam te non sospite gentes
posse magis, sine te quam possim ego, pascere vitam?

There may be greener vales and hills
    Less bare to shelter man;
But still they want the naiad rills
    And miss the pipe of Pan.

There may be other isles as fair
    And summer seas as blue,
But then Odysseus touched not there,
    Nor Argo beached her crew.

For me the Nereid-haunted shore,
    The Faun-frequented dell,
Can wake the note of wonder more
    Than stones where Caesars fell.

LORD RENNELL OF RODD

Si magis his alibi sunt antra virentia, si sunt
    protectura suos his iuga nuda minus,
desunt multa tamen; plorant sine naide rivi;
    non ibi dat notos Panis avena modos.
Insula si similis procul est eademque venustas,
    ridet et aestivi par color ille maris,
istuc nulla tamen Minyas advexerat Argo,
    non ea Dulichiam senserat ora ratem.
Me mea Nereisin celeberrima litora tangunt,
    me quod amat crebro Faunus obire nemus.
Horum est miranti potius compellere vocem
    quam si Caesaribus stant monumenta necis.

So playful Love on Ida's flowery sides
With ribbon-rein the indignant lion guides;
Pleased on his brindled back the lyre he rings,
And shakes delirious rapture from the strings.
Soft nymphs on timid step the triumph view,
And listening fauns with beating hoofs pursue;
With pointed ears the alarmed forest starts,
And love and music soften savage hearts.

DARWIN

Talis Amor vehitur ludens in floribus Idae,
    et subit indignans mollia frena leo.
Terga iubaeque placent; divina insania chordis
    excutitur, sumptam dum ferit arte lyram.
Dant sonitum pedibus fauni numerosque sequuntur;
    lenta dryas timide spectat ovare deum.
Sentit silva pavens, et acutas arrigit aures;
    et fera cantando pectora mollit Amor.

She dwelt among us till the flowers, 'tis said,
  Grew jealous of her. With precipitate feet,
As loth to wrong them unawares, she fled.
  Earth is less fragrant now, and Heaven more sweet.

WILLIAM WATSON

ἄνθεσιν Ἄνθις, φασίν, ἐπίφθονος οὖσα παρ' ἡμῖν
  οὐ μάλα δὴν ἔμενεν μή τι λαθοῦσ' ἀδικῇ,
ἀλλὰ θοοῖς προφθᾶσ' ἀπέδρα ποσίν· αὐτίκα δ' ὄζει
  τἀκεῖ θ' ἡδύτερον τἀνθάδε τ' οὐ τὸ πάρος.

E. L. V.

Farewell, my tutor. Still in memories
  Your kindness shines like sunlight slanting through
Dim rooms to brighten fading tapestries;
  And all your gray-haired boys are mourning you.

LORD DUNSANY

Tutor, ave atque vale. Priscos reparare colores
pallida in obscuro pendentia pariete texta
solis ad obliquam lucem quo more videmus,
ista animi bonitas memori sic lumine fulget.
Nos, tua turba, senescentes ploramus ademptum.

AD IONAM NVBENTEM

a.d. viii Id. Apr.

Here anemones, half awake,
Shake acold in the naked brake;
Here is hardly a bird to sing,
Hardly here is a voice of spring,
   Joan my daughter, to greet you.

Yet the poet is full aware
Bells are joyfully pealing there,
There the roads and the houses shine
All with daisy and celandine,
   Joan, to welcome and meet you.

So he sends to you o'er the long
Counties, lifted on wings of song,
Harnessed lightly in dancing rhyme,
Prayer and blessing and hope sublime,
   Joan, my Joan, to attend you.

Bright and beautiful be your way;
Yours be all that I think or say;
Love be with you from all you know;
Love be with you where'er you go;
   Love, my daughter, I send you.

Hic tremunt anemonides
nuda per nemora algidae
vix aperto oculo; tibi hic
nulla quae canat est avis,
    nulla vocula veris.
Scit poeta tuus tamen
quot procul resonent lyrae,
quae te bellis, Iona, quae
te chelidonia in domo
    per viasque salutet.
Aptat in numeros leves
quod volet super Angliam
canticum: pia vota te
prosequantur, Iona, te
    spes ab aethere fulgens.
Pulchra sint tibi laetaque et
quot volo bona vel loquor;
sis beata, ubicunque eris,
caritatibus omnium,
    cara filia nobis.

O thou that from thy mansion,
   Through time and place to roam,
Dost send abroad thy children,
   And then dost call them home,

That men and tribes and nations
   And all thy hand hath made
May shelter them from sunshine
   In thine eternal shade:

We now to peace and darkness
   And earth and thee restore
Thy creature that thou madest
   And wilt cast forth no more.

A. E. HOUSMAN

O quicunque tua sede deus procul
oras progeniem mittis in exteras,
hoc errare quod est temporis aut loci,
    mox idem revocas domum

tecum perpetua nocte recolligens
haec ipsis manibus quae facis omnia,
seu gentes hominum seu populos creas,
    lumen solis ut arceant:

ergo nunc tenebris atque silentio
tellurique simul reddimus et tibi
hoc quod de nihilo condideras opus
    nec post eicies foras.

FOR GREEK VERSE

Lady, I came not in the idle hope
That words of mine would fall as summer rain
Upon the furrows of thy fruitless grief
And nurse thee back to the sun and to sweet life.
There is a fulness of calamity,
And when one holds it, sense no more abides
Either of touching hand or spoken word;
But like to iron or to stubborn stone
The mind stands still, and night falls on the eyes,
And all the doors of thought are closed.

οὔτοι, γύναι, παρῆλθον ἐλπίσας μάτην
ὡς θερινὸν ὄμβρον τἀμὰ ῥήματ' ἂν πεσεῖν
τῆς σῆς ἀκάρπου πημονῆς ἐπ' αὔλακας
τρέφοντ' ἐς ἥλιόν σε καὶ γλυκὺν βίον.
ἤτοι πέλει τις πλησμονὴ τῶν ξυμφορῶν,
ὅταν δ' ἔχῃ τις, οὐκέτ' αἴσθησις μένει
προσθιγγανούσης χειρὸς ἢ ῥητοῦ λόγου,
ἀλλ' ὡσπερεὶ σίδηρος ἢ λίθου δίκην
ἕστηκε φρήν, καὶ νὺξ ὄρωρ' ἐπ' ὀμμάτων,
καὶ ξυγκέκληται πᾶσα φροντίδων θύρα.

FOR LATIN VERSE

I

Ambition rolls her car
  Where roars the crowded town,
And seeks in dust of war
  The loud road of renown.
But Wisdom keeps her glade
  Where crystal water flows,
And walks in quiet shade
  Among the lily and rose.

II

From mountain top he sees the land;
And all its wondrous wealth is scanned.

Broad rivers in the valleys run;
Great crops stand golden in the sun.

The vine and olive thickly grow;
The meads with milk and honey flow.

'Adieu', he cries, 'most fair to see,
'Land of my race, not mine to be.'

AUGUST

Now runs the silly season
  When masters are at play
And every petty treason
  Must up and have its say.

In the unguarded stable
  The mongrel leaves his bone
And takes the manger, able
  For once to hold his own.

And lovely things and olden,
  Discovered to the few
And from the rest withholden,
  Are loveless as the new.

Now is the season running
  When stones and mud are thrown,
And men of little cunning,
  Unknowing, make it known.

A THOUGHT

A golden fancy gliding
   Beside me softly steals
As I go gaily riding
   On silent wheels—
In shadow disappearing,
   And then in chequered light
Shining again and veering
   From dark to bright.

I may not look too closely
   For fear it then escape;
Or stain with vision grossly
   The fairy shape.
In dusk of dreamland shrouded,
   Or lapped in pools of day,
It passes, clear or clouded,
   Here and away.

If it be lost to vision,
   The mind remembering
Will save in clean precision
   The shining thing.
The joy that has no measure,
   The more than golden mean,
To see is briefer pleasure
   Than to have seen.

LOVE AND SERVICE

Lover and servant, not on fame or fee
Dependent shall thy love and service be.

This be thy cause and promise, evermore
To guard thy lovely lady, and adore.

And though she come in gold and silver shower,
Herself shall be thy joy, and not her dower.

And if all poor and naked she appear,
No less thou shalt embrace and hold her dear.

And daily shall thy treasure-house be stored;
For Love and Service are their own reward.

ΕΠΙΣΤΗΜΗ ΕΠΙΣΤΗΜΗΣ

Said Dickon, searching for the spring
Of actual knowledge, 'Blow it!
'I find that, though I know a thing,
'I cannot know I know it.'

THE NOVICE

To show the varlets from the start
How hard his hand and stout his heart,
A Reign of Terror Tupkins made;
No man was ever more afraid.

JEUNESSE DORÉE

O you who think in milliards
　　And live for sport and victuals,
For port wine and billiards,
　　Or beer at least and skittles,

Prepare for disappointment
　　In bitter days to come;
A fly is in the ointment,
　　A powder in the plum.

TO SOMEBODY

I would not for the world say anything to hurt you,
　　Or use an expression you might not think was nice;
But if you must make a necessity of virtue,
　　How is your freedom unallied with vice?

BOLTON ABBEY

Here I sprawl on flowered green,
    Where the waters drawl and run;
    All I had to do is done;
All that was to be has been.

Thought, be near; but only peep
    Round the corner. Let me lie
    Scarcely knowing thou art nigh;
Wake me not, nor let me sleep.

Memory alone has place.
    Silent as the sunlight, still
    As a distant town or hill,
She shall stand before my face.

She shall stand in vesture bright,
    Wonderful, and fair to see;
    As I frame her shall she be,
Made by me for my delight.

HAREBELLS

Flowers of the wayside, delicate and diaphanous,
    Trembling and shivering in the airless noon,
Coloured more lucently than opal or than amethyst,
    Shall I be sorrowful that you pass so soon?

Nay. If your beauty were permanent and inviolate,
    Not so alluringly would it hold my eyes.
Hateful to man is the thought of long satiety;
    Dearer the vision of the thing that dies.

RED TAPE

Red tape is the thing
   When you wish to say No;
It's tighter than string
   And doesn't let go.

Some speak of elastic
   And similar stuff
As being more plastic
   Though equally tough.

But you cannot escape
   From what I have said;
There's nothing like tape,
   Provided it's red.

Red tape will enable
   You always to lay
Your cards on the table
   And never to play.

When high you sit,
   A master of men,
To exact or remit
   With stroke of pen,

From all who tease you
   With hard demands
Red tape frees you
   By tying your hands.

THE BULLY

Lifted to awful power from common birth,
    As made of adamant he takes his stand,
And, loosing hideous havoc o'er the earth,
    Pleads that a little people forced his hand.

SALISBURY

Are you walking with me
    In this garden green,
    Seeing, yet unseen?
Are you talking with me,
    Giving word for word,
    Hearing, yet unheard?

Did you stay beside me
    In the house of prayer?
    At the altar there
Did you pray beside me?
    Though I know not how,
    Do you touch me now?

Not the knowing of it
    Could be more intense
    Than this present sense,
Nor the showing of it
    Make it clearer to me,
    Bring you nearer to me.

THE DEAD HAND

Because we walk on hallowed ground
Where hushed is every common sound,

And man will readily forgive
Rather the dead than those who live,

And, further, the accused is dumb
And may not to his trial come

Nor passing from his other place
Meet his accuser face to face—

By honoured custom, of the dead
Nothing but good is rightly said.

But you—You *wrote* the words of doom;
And none can tax you in the tomb.

For this there is no hallowed ground,
For this no remedy is found,

When, from his cold and distant bed,
Ill of the living speaks the dead.

THE SLIP

I am the slip that Gubbins made;
I throw his merits in the shade;
No flight of time shall make me fade,
    Or rust of custom stain;
The like of me is hard to seek;
I am the very point and peak
Of all he did. I am unique.
    He never slipped again.

For fifty years he ruled the state,
And all acclaimed him good and great.
Poor man, he little knew his fate,
    Or what he'd leave behind.
And now, however long you look
Throughout however many a book,
Though resolute with hook and crook,
    You'll find him hard to find.

The laws he framed, the wars he won,
The empire that outstripped the sun,
The nothing that he left undone,
    Are dead, or soon will die;
But once he perpetrated me,
Once only made an error. He
For this shall unforgotten be.
    His monument am I.

POST MORTEM

I often supposed when I talked on earth
That much that I said was of solid worth;
But Lord! I am filled with immoderate pride
At the words they have put in my mouth since I died.

OCTOBER

Now Magdalene in the morning
   Is standing dark and still,
A figure in flat shading
   For coloured brush to fill;
Then comes the sun, adorning
   Low roof and linden glade,
And Magdalene in the morning
   Is why the world was made.

For Magdalene in October
   Is glorious to behold,
And all her simple raiment
   Is dipped in rose and gold.
All sombre things and sober
   Are not for me this morn,
For Magdalene in October
   Is why a man was born.

J'Y SUIS, J'Y RESTE

Immovable Hugh has little to do,
  And little he seems to regret it;
'It's pleasanter, what? to keep what is got
  'Than ever it was to get it.'

He sits on his pile and continues to smile:
  'My friends, you may take it from me,
'It's easier far to stay where you are
  'Than anywhere else', says he.

'One point from the ten deduct, and you then
  'Will find the remainder is nine;
'You may stand as a stone on feet of your own,
  'But that which I sit on is mine.'

CONSISTENCY

'Nothing but good of the dead', says Ned
  To those who are unforgiving;
And nothing but good says he of the dead,
  And nothing but bad of the living.

NOSEY PARKER

Why the plants so finely grow
In my garden, what I throw
On them, that they thickly blow,
Nosey Parker wants to know.

* * * *

Why the plants so finely grew
In my garden, what I threw
On them, that they thickly blew,
Nosey Parker never knew.

NOVEMBER

As through a rich man's chamber,
  Along the covered floor
On cloth of chrome and amber
  I pass from door to door

By arras frayed and faded
  Of darkling stem and wand,
And threaded all and braided
  With form of golden frond.

Attended by such beauty
  In early morning calm
I pass to daily duty
  Of prayer and rede and psalm;

And saints in heaven shall hold me
  Not thankless, knowing well
The half that was not told me
  Is more than I can tell.

Q.E.D.

The International Institute of Intellectual Cooperation
    Met and deliberated in a capital city,
And decided that the habit of intellectual isolation
    Was, to say the least of it, a lamentable pity.

So they very soon arrived at a unanimous resolution
    That only an intellectual cooperation,
Arrived at by an international institution,
    Could benefit this or any other nation.

And, further, they decided it was wholly ineffectual,
    And in fact beyond a question quite irrational,
To think of cooperation unless it was intellectual
    Or of any institution other than international.

R.K.

Importunity, undefeated angel,
Fly post-haste to the house of Antoninus,
Kiss him, fondle him, hang your arms about him,
Make him come to us, howsoe'er reluctant.
Though ten times he decline the invitation,
Ask him twenty or thirty times or forty,
Ask him fifty or sixty times or eighty;
Then most charmingly multiply the total,
Till, enchanted, he comes to Magdalena,
Comes enchanted to lovely Magdalena,
Where our company, eager-eyed, awaits him.

NON-PARTY

I am an Independent,
  I am quite open-minded,
  I am never blinded
By whatever is in the ascendant.

Every Englishman inherits
  A right to hold an opinion
  Under nobody's dominion
And to judge every case on its merits.

Besides, it is less worrying
  If others without winking
  Are doing the thinking
And all the hurrying and scurrying.

Furthermore, in my blinkers
  My votes I may double,
  And without any trouble;
For not a few are the non-thinkers.

DECEMBER

Rose of Lancaster, lone and fair,
Hanging red in the wintry air,
Glowing amid the brown and bare,

Go to a loved and kingly place,
Praying its lord to let you grace
His hand to-day for a little space.

Eton and King's are triumphing:
This is the birthday of their king;
Magdalene, too, may softly sing.

Magdalene, too,—and none will frown—
May, lowly, lay her tribute down,
A rosebud in the red rose crown.

JANUARY

Where my bright hearth is blazing
  I stand, and turn my eyes
Where dazing and amazing
  The white snow flies,
And decked in a strange splendour
  Magdalene lies.

He laughs at all mischancing
  Who watches the white snow,
Prancing and entrancing,
  Fly to and fro,
And downward flow and downward
  Downward flow.

How blessed to behold it
  Silent on Magdalene fall,
Enfold it and hold it
  In scarf and shawl;
Lost are the other senses;
  Seeing is all.

THE HUMAN BOY

The platitudes about education,
    Which experience has shown to be so true,
Have been repeated to me in endless reiteration
    For forty years and two.

But though they are all but unassailable,
    And impossible, I grant you, to deny,
Oft when the living test of them is available,
    Then are they blown sky-high.

For in spite of your pedagogues and professors,
    And systems psychologically sound,
To say nothing of the theorists and the window-dressers
    On every platform found,

No multitude of formulas and set phrases
    Can suppress, thank God, the laughing boys at school;
You might as well bid the buttercups and the daisies
    To spring by book and rule.

FEBRUARY

Up the sun in splendour goes
 From the white fields of dawn;
Pencilling of trees he throws
 Along the silvered lawn.

Kindled in the garden grey
 The hazel pendants gleam;
Magdalene lies alight with day,
 Yet half in shade and dream.

So in chequered dark and bright
 My pleasant lines are laid,
Fired anew with orient light
 And soft with lovely shade.

MAY

When May is lavishing all his treasure,
  Filling the measure to overflowing,
Ravishing the senses with colour and scent,
  Snowing and snowing
The orchard with showers of flowers,
  Flooding the eyes with the wonderment
Of lakes of bluebells and bannered lilac and
  flags in glory of purple ascending—

When this beatitude holds me captured,
  Holds me enraptured and dumb, confessing
Gratitude in silence, and simply receiving
  Blessing on blessing
In rivers that flow and o'erflow,
  Feasted, I feast, nor am unbelieving
In joy eternal and perfect beauty and
  sight unsated in vision unending.

IN DULCI IUVENTA

Follies of youth—
    We that outlive them
Know of a truth
    God will forgive them,

All that was bad in them
    Fading away,
Good that we had in them
    Living to-day.

VT TEREBRAS

What you tell me, Sir Ernest Bore,
    Of the life of the average sow—
I never knew it before,
    Nor know if I know it now.

MAGDALENE

Come whatever Muse thou art
That singest of content of heart,
Be near me and indite the verse
In number, if I dare rehearse
The passing hours and count in rhyme
Those pleasing measured steps of time
That lightly fall from dusk of dawn
Till instantly dun Sleep has drawn
His curtain. All the livelong day
My tongue would shape a roundelay
And fasten it to stop or string
Had I the skill to play or sing.
Daily here is gladness born
Whenas in prayer at early morn
The two or three together meet;
Anon the hours on feathered feet
Trip, and Doctrine and Discipline
Go side by side, and scholars win
Reproof or praise, whether their eyes
Scan the emended exercise,
Or from their youthful lips are rolled
The thunders that were heard of old.
Then to the court, where all is gay
In the dividing of the day,
And books and gowns are laid aside
For merry ease at luncheon-tide,
And smiling face and cheerful voice
Salute me. Proudly I rejoice
Over this tribute given free
Of friendship and of courtesy,
And gaily turn my steps, and so
To careful Clerk or Bursar go,

Or beg of patient President
Or Tutor that their ears be lent
In counsel; and perchance I see
To somewhat at the Buttery,
And so return to food and leisure.
   Soon it may be my deep-set pleasure—
Save when the shire in session calls,
Or syndics within sunless walls,
Or menace to the country-side—
To ride on silent wheels, and be
In Harlton or in Madingley,
Or Knapwell's flowered brake, or by
Willow and water and mirrored sky.
And dear returns the old delight
Wakened at the sound and sight
Of boys who, bearing Magdalene's name,
On river or field, in race or game,
Extend their strength and all but die
In high and generous rivalry.
For boy and man in perfect kind
Are built of body no less than mind,
And games inform the unwrit sense
Of friendship's fine intelligence.
Now evening comes with essay heard,
Or admonition's kindest word,
Or book or pen, till punctual bell
Calls to pious service. Well
I love the ordered life expressed
In worship and the Name confessed
By this our family, old and young,
With lesson, and petition sung
To Guide and Guardian. Thence to Hall,
Where ancient grace and ritual
Hallow the common meal, and hold
The passing years in harness. Cold
Were life unclad in ancestry
Of manners and Time's livery,

And is the richer if it shine
With mirthful talk and the red wine
Of France or Douro. When too soon
The hour has struck, my mind immune
Plays with itself a little space,
Or boys have gathered, and we pace
The sceptred stage of Sophocles;
Or, rare delight, the ranks are set,
And at the chequered board are met
Assailant and defender; till
Dustman comes at last to fill
Reluctant eyes; and so to bed,
Where scarcely have I laid my head
On pillow, when the happy day
Into dreamland fades away,
Till all this bliss once more is born,
And Magdalene 'waits me in the morn.

WAR

I

Now is the time when little things
    Are nothing. Now with stone and stock
We stand once more and the clean springs
    That well forth from the rock.

Now we are washed of mud and dust,
    And speak the truth, and cast away
The clammy trammels of distrust
    In the large air of day.

How sooty and grimëd now appear
    Faction and quarrel. How sublime
The lifted Cause, and Hope most dear
    Mounting the stairs of Time.

Only the small will creep and prick,
    When hearts are great and England stands
With eyes that watch in darkness thick
    And swift and armëd hands.

WAR

II

You poor little mealy mouthy man,
　　Maybe you cannot truly help yourself;
I care not if you cannot or you can;
　　You should be put away upon a shelf.

You should be in a cupboard, locked away
　　With all your dirty little politics;
What use can England have for you to-day,
　　You and your soiled and greasy bag of tricks?

These are the days when truly noble birth
　　Is seen among the high or lowly born,
And meanness is revealed for what it's worth
　　And earns the scholar's and the soldier's scorn.

WAR

III

NOTHING NEW

In earth's primaeval state no other law
Held good but that of tooth and beak and claw;
The beasts had found how fruitful was your plan
Or e'er appeared on earth the face of man.

And that whereof you claim the fatherhood
Was common form ere yet the city stood,
And far away in days of stick and stone
The furtive and the false were not unknown.

WAR

IV

The glory and guerdon
  To men who are older;
  But ours is to shoulder
The weight of the burden.

More stubborn, and younger,
  We stick it, remaining
  At home, and restraining
Our thirst and our hunger

For blood and for battle,
  While brothers and cousins
  And uncles by dozens
Are slaughtered like cattle.

The lantern of learning,
  Unfed by the prudent
  And national student,
Might cease from its burning.

And therefore we nerve us
  To shoulder the burden,
  Regardless of guerdon
If England preserve us.

WAR

V

Dismal Jemmy, why regret
Ills that haven't happened yet?
Better keep a moan or two
For the prospect when it's blue.

Disappointed we shall be
When the earth and heavens flee,
If upon that aweful day
You have nothing more to say.

THOU SHALT NOT

God knows I am no warrior,
  To march or sail or fly;
Never was born a sorrier
  Man militant than I.

And kind but firm civility
  To me has made it plain
That men of my agility
  Will keep the watch in vain.

Yet England, though a million
  She arm for battle hot,
Has that which one civilian
  May help by doing not.

He shall not heed unverified
  And dismal things to hear,
Or fables of the terrified,
  Nor foul his lips with fear.

And, with dark looks and sinister,
  To pour the easy blame
On strategist and minister
  He shall account it shame.

PURPUREUM VER

Flora from her golden cup
Heaps the hues and odours up;
Seven times the rainbow's seven
Colours breathe the airs of heaven.

Yellow locks and glittering braid
Break in cresset and cascade;
Pearl and purple, uplifted high,
Stream across the azure sky.

Amethyst and ruby strew
Floor and bank, and, deep in blue
Mist, the standing stems uphold
Orbs of amber and globes of gold.

Not more glorious can appear
City seen of heavenly seer,
Where on portal and wall divine
Sardius and sapphire shine.

If undying life be won
When the days on earth are done,
Not incomparable with this
Be, for me, the unfading bliss.

LINGVA PRAECOX

Young man, you know not what you say;
   You talk as though you were still at school.
'How', you will moan in a later day,
   'Could I have been such a staring fool?'

When others are young, and you are old,
   And high their talk through head and hat,
A clammy fear may strike you cold:
   'I, when I talked, did I look like that?'

H.B.

That rather jolly rum-looking fellow over there,
So kind to all and some, so warm and debonair,
As fat as a plum and as soft as a slug—
His Christian name is Hum, and his surname is Bug.

KNAPWELL

Seeing is belief where the pale flowers are blowing
  Thick through the wood as far as eye may see,
Lovelier than thought, and known but to the knowing,
  Known in this noon and seen of none but me.

Near me there is none to stand staring and drinking
  Draughts of delight, a thirst for ever filled—
Wishing and possessing, thought without the thinking,
  Treasure for the having, thrown about and spilled.

Lavishly created and cast down about me,
  Feeding my eyes in one of a few hours—
Now would it be wasted and purposeless without me;
  I am the Cause of this great floor of flowers.

HISTORY

When the written document
Proved him wise and innocent,

Rumour only laughed and said
'I am twenty days ahead;

'Now the truth may pound away,
Labouring with feet of clay:

'I shall multiply the lie
Till the earth and heavens die.'

A DIAGNOSIS

This case is slightly different from that of the majority,
  This illusion under which MacDoodle labours;
It's a most decided complex of acute inferiority,
  Not in himself, but in his friends and neighbours.

ΜΙΣΩ ΜΝΑΜΟΝΑ

My thoughts of Parkinson are far from lenient,
  And if he asks the reason, he shall know;
His memory is very inconvenient;
  He tells you what you said a week ago.

IN COUNCIL

Mr Partipolitix,
How he brays and how he kicks!
'Red is red, and blue is blue;
I am I, and you are you;
Half a dozen isn't six.

Join with others? Fiddlesticks!
Oil and acid cannot mix;
Black is black, and white is white;
You are wrong, and I am right;
I am Partipolitix.'

How he pries, and how he pricks!
What a peck of holes he picks!
Nothing is too good to hate,
Or too crooked to be straight,
Nothing loose he cannot fix.

Up is he to tons of tricks,
Splashing mud and shying bricks;
How he twists the moral laws,
How he hees and hums and haws,
Mr Partipolitix!

NE PASSERONT PAS

'They shall not pass! They shall not pass!' he cried,
And answering legions faced the fire, and died.
He lived, and, later, crawling from the grave,
Surrendered what his soldiers died to save.

RIGHT ABOUT

He saw no other course was left
But that of murder, lies, and theft;
If sinless is the Muscovite,
It follows that the left is right.

NOT SO BAD

'Old Thingumabob isn't fit for his job,'
  You tell me, 'He's making a mess of it';
And ever you carp at him sharply, and harp
  On a string; and I wish I had less of it.

You bitterly talk of his voice and his walk
  And his teeth and his nose and the rest of him;
But parts of him seem to deserve our esteem,
  And I am for making the best of him.

ΓΝΩΘΙ ΣΕΑΥΤΟΝ

I have been careful to assess
  My talents. If another man
Appraise me, he must grope and guess.
  I know myself. None other can.

If I excelled in anything,
  That excellence to me is known,
Such secret treasure as a king
  Locks in a chamber of his own.

SELF-PITY

Deceiver, get behind me!
  I loathe those piteous eyes
And lips that would remind me
  Of fancied miseries.

Thy sighs that thus importune
  Ere now have been the bane
Of golden sons of Fortune,
  And shall be yet again.

INTERPRETES DEORVM

O ye who stand upon the starry floors,
  Blame not our praise of those who, here and there,
  Loosing the songs of heaven on lower air,
Open for us the everlasting doors.

GARDE TA FOY

When a little more or less
Tilts the balance of success,
When a little less or more
Scares the Terror from the door,
GARDE TA FOY

Many men, and some the best,
Come not to the fiery test;
Others once, and once alone,
Meet it, and their worth is shown.
GARDE TA FOY

Use disarms, and ev'n the wise
Oft are taken by surprise;
Men of thousand actions done
Faithless have been proved by one.
GARDE TA FOY

When the lure is winning, when
Thou art all but fallen, then,
Innocent and proud, recall
Where was writ upon the wall
GARDE TA FOY

FROM CATULLUS

Yesterday at leisure
On my tablets, quaffing
Cups of wine and laughing,
Did we play, such pretty
Pastime was our pleasure,
Paying scores in witty
Verse of varied measure.
All my soul was burning
With the merry fashion
Of thy wit and learning,
So that I returning
Could not tame my passion,
Food and slumber scorning,
Turning, ever turning
O'er my couch and yearning
For the light of morning,
With the expectation
Of thy conversation.
When my poor bed languished
With my tossing on it,
And my limbs were lying
Very like to dying,
Then I made this sonnet,
So thou mightest gather
How my heart is anguished.
Be not unattending,
Neither rash; but rather
Hear, oh hear my crying.
Nemesis descending
(Have a care, for heavy
Is her hand) may levy
Toll on thy offending.

VITA SENIS

Let him have books when near the end,
A house and garden, bed, and friend,
Wine, and a fire by which to nod,
A merry heart and the love of God.

THE REPEATER

The same thing in a single day
So many times does Harper say,
Full certainly the drift were caught
Of what he thinks, if e'er he thought.

MICHAELMAS AT ETON

ANTE THRONVM DOMINI

Where the Lord is throned on high,
Loud you sing the victory,
  Angels, in the heavenly hall;
Standing in our hallowed fane,
Lift we here the joyful strain—
  'God and England!' sing we all.

Mighty Michael captains you,
Who the dragon overthrew,
  Michael crowned with victory;
We shall follow in the fray
Where his banner points the way—
  'God and England!' is our cry.

Now with drawn protecting sword
Guard the children of the Lord,
  Guard us with unfailing sight;
Now we arm us for the foe,
Then shall into battle go,
  Then for God and England fight.

Where you stand with lilies crowned,
Robed in white, your harps resound
  With celestial melody;
So we stand in raiment white,
So our joyous hymn recite—
  'God and England! Victory!'

Hark, the trumpets blown on high,
Hark, the triumph in the sky,
  And our voices answering;
Song from children's lips outpoured
Praises and adores the Lord—
  'God and England!' loud we sing.

HOMO OMNIPOTENS

Others let their mind react
To experience and fact,
Draw conclusions, and at last
Nail their colours to the mast.

Tomkins does the nailing first,
Likes to have the thing reversed,
Takes his premise and to it
Makes event and action fit.

Mighty names that please him not
From the record will he blot;
Caesar is erased with scorn;
Bonaparte was never born.

In opponents if it be,
Faith is infidelity;
If the assassin he approve,
Murder is an act of love.

God himself, the poets say,
Cannot alter yesterday,
Cannot make the lot of man
Not have fallen. Tomkins can.

Tomkins has acquired a greater
Function than his own Creator;
Ill content with *Let there be*,
'Let there not have been', says he.

NON-STOP

Mrs Chitterchatterbox
Chatters like a dozen clocks;
While the Councillors debate
Highest themes of realm and state,
Merrily she ticks and tocks.

'Have you seen my holly-hocks?
Poor old Jerry 's on the rocks.
Who's that ranting over there?
Percy Perkins, I declare!
How I hate the dirty fox!'

So she sits, and so she mocks,
Wags her tongue and shakes her locks.
'What to me are rate and rent,
Fact and figure, argument,
Debt, and empty money-box?

Why attend to cranks and crocks
Crowing like a lot of cocks?
If I choose to chit and chatter,
What the dickens does it matter?
I am Chitterchatterbox.'

DISTINGVO

In this at least we saw
    They differed—God and Brown:
The one set up the law,
    The other laid it down.

ANTIPATHY

'Mike,'
Said Peters,
'I dislike.
First,
He's cursed
With a stammer. Next,
I am vexed
By his laugh; and thirdly,
He talks so absurdly
And endlessly. Lastly,
He's ghastly.'

WISH AND THOUGHT

To Brown the sky must be always blue,
For what he wishes he thinks is true.

ΤΗΝ ΚΑΤΑ ΣΑΥΤΟΝ ΕΛΑ

From pillar to post the Professor, perplext,
  Need never have galloped so fast,
Deserting his latest defence for his next,
  If only he'd stuck to his last.

CLEON

JUNE 1940

Had I been there
   With ship and gun,
   The furious Hun
   Had cut and run—
Had I been there.

I hated war
   When not too old
   To be enrolled
   Among the bold—
I hated war.

Now I am older,
   'Advance!' I cry,
   'With courage high
   'To do and die'—
Now I am older.

The dirty cowards
   Who dared it not—
   I'd sack the lot,
   Or have them shot—
The dirty cowards.

Had I been there,
   I'd stormed the town,
   And done it brown,
   And knocked it down,
Had I been there.

THE SIGN OF THREE

That Jesus, son of Sirach, said
A man's true nature may be read
In dress and gait and laugh alone,
And all of him by these be known,
That poor young donkey over there
Presumably is not aware.

JUVENILIA

I

LOVE AND DEATH

With pulse of rose and azure wings,
    And piteous failing hands,
And eyes where wondrous sorrow springs,
    Love at his doorway stands.

And still with lifted arm of might,
    And heavy feet of doom,
Death storms the house alive with light
    And sweet with summer bloom.

No crown he wears. Whoso can face
    Those eyes nor pay them heed,
Unmastered by their tender grace,
    Is more than king indeed.

JUVENILIA

II

O wondrous blue abysmal eyes
Like spaces deep in summer skies:
O sight incomparably fair:
The secret of the world is there.

No other sound or sight is worth
That silent speech of sudden mirth,
When swiftly in a moment breaks
Bright laughter, and your soul awakes.

The earth is dark and cold and vile,
And, lo, you lift your face, and smile,
And rays of light celestial fall,
And Heaven is round us after all.

JUVENILIA

III

Pan started from a sleep of pain,
And saw the frost on hill and plain;
He smote the ground with shining rain
    And filled the woods with flowers.

With flowing vein and tingling limb,
The red wrath at his nostril's brim,
He stirred the great earth under him
    With suns and winds and showers.

The grass shone clear; the buds began
To lift their lids and peep at Pan;
Loud the streams rejoicing ran,
    And music broke from the bowers.

THE THREE CS

When I look back along the track,
    Then to myself I say
'My blessing be on pastimes three
    I found beside the way—

The unfolded golden books of old,
    Open and ever young,
And art that went on instrument
    Of Greek or Latin tongue—

The name and fame of England's game,
    The sunny hours afield,
The lasting friendships to the end,
    In noble conflict sealed—

The fretted set of fawn and jet,
    The mind alive, alight,
The gleaming board, the roads explored
    Beyond the range of sight.'

These three I bless, and not the less
    For that, to like them well,
A man might take them for their sake,
    Nor had he to excel.

ARMCHAIRING

The man in the street through rain and through sleet
Delivers his views on the army and fleet,
And casts his opinions to wind and to air.
Mine are more weighty; they come from the Chair.

THE BROAD VIEW

You say that the wider my notion is spread
The more will reject it. The nail on the head!
I have known it indeed from my earliest youth—
The greater the distance the dimmer the truth.

FRONS LAETA PARVM

What is that trouble on thy youthful brow,
   No longer lifted to the joy of living?
   What at my heart the chill touch of misgiving?
Thou wert my joy and light and pride. And now

Thou art Marcellus, and about thy head
   I see the shade of death, and know the unspoken
   Dread of the hard arbitrament unbroken.
Vain gifts my hands may scatter o'er the dead

Of lily or violet soon. Ah me, alas
   That thus the beauty of man, and all we cherish
   Of what is lovely and adorable, may perish
As flow'rs of the field shorn down or as the grass.

TRUTH

To those who fix their eyes
  On Truth's immaculate form
The whiter for the frowning skies
  She shows against the storm.

To those who gravely scan
  The lines on memory's page
And read how stood the upright man
  In frenzies of his age—

To them dark calumnies
  Only illume his name;
The thicker round him breed the lies,
  The fairer shines his fame.

And he—high scorn he throws
  At poisoned tongue and tooth,
And asks to judge him only those
  Who care to learn the truth.

EDUCATION

It is fundamental to the good of the community
    To coordinate the many cultural activities
And, obliterating inequalities of opportunity,
    To provide a common basis for proclivities:
Which has led us to the inevitable conviction
    That, as soon as England has recovered from the storm,
The removal of all administrative restriction
    Is a necessary precondition of reform.

The appropriate authorities of all localities,
    Bearing in mind the principles of sociology
In respect of economic potentialities
    (Which is merely a matter of expert methodology),
Should facilitate the essential consideration
    Of whatever influence or aspect they may deem
To be a unit capable of integration
    Within the content of a statutory scheme.

And in order that the system may be nationalised,
    And nothing militate against its generality,
The relationship of institutions should be rationalised
    On a plan to be determined in totality;
And attention then should tend to be directed
    To the implementing of a regulated sphere
Where every idiosyncrasy is intersected
    And all the differentiations disappear.

CAMBRIDGE

Many works of man are his shame, and at their perishing
  Only of refreshment shall be heard the sigh;
Many have been wrought for our clasping and our cherishing,
  Loveliness its lovers will defend from death or die.

Pyramids may crumble in ruin undeplorable,
  Babylons may vanish, unwept, beyond recall;
Heavenly Jerusalems and Parthenons adorable,
  These men have fallen for, fiercely, lest they fall.

City of remembrance, where once we walked delightfully,
  Where not a door of paradise was barred,
Stricken be the hands that can handle thee despitefully,
  Blinded be the eyes that can see thy beauty scarred.

Garden, court and hall in thee, and pleasant paths of piety—
  Fields of companionship ever young and green—
Seats of high intercourse and loveliest society—
  Such as we have seen thee, forever be thou seen.

Distantly, enchantingly, a splendour is shed over thee,
  Falling on the lawns and the waters at thy feet;
Woven of Desire are the glorious robes that cover thee;
  Holiness and Beauty within thy palace meet.

Whoso lays mischievous hands upon thy royalty,
  Staining indecently thy noble face and dress,
Darkness be his noon in the sin of his disloyalty,
  Powder be his rain in the day of his distress.

God from all gentleness and from all comfort sunder him;
  Cursëd be his basket and cursëd be his store;
Brass be his heaven above his head, and under him
  Iron his earth, that hour and evermore.

FROM MIMNERMUS

Even as the leaves which swell beneath the sun,
  By spring engendered in the flowering time,
  Like unto them, rejoicing in our prime,
We bloom but for a span, and knowledge none

Have we of ill from heaven or of boon.
  Near by our side dark Destinies do stand,
  And the twin dooms they hold in either hand
Of painful eld or death; and passing soon

Is youth's enjoyment, lasting but a day;
  And when the flower is gone, to die is best,
  For thick the troubles follow. Goods possessed
Are lost, and cometh aching Want to stay,

Or sickness keepeth body and spirit low;
  And some are childless and for children crave,
  And, craving still, go down into the grave.
To one and all God giveth woe on woe.

PROOF

Nothing may come to those who wait,
A fool and his money be parted late,
In union very weakness be,
And best of company be three;
I've known a poet made, not born;
I've seen a rose without a thorn,
Jones unsoothed by music, Smith
Lacking what to meddle with.
Proverbs are true, but any fool
Knows the exception proves the rule.

ABIIT AD PLURES

MacDuff had a nose for the side
   That was winning, and gave it priority,
And, still on the scent as he died,
   Turned over and joined the majority.

GENTLEMEN

True gentlemen of England, when she bleeds,
   Go side by side, scornful of party strife,
   And holding nought more precious than her life
They count no words as mightier than deeds.

For England's sake they utter not complaint
   Of daily hardship. Silently they pay
   Their service; and to use her disarray
For other ends they deem the foulest taint.

APOLOGIA

Undone has been my duty,
My sins are past forgiving,
But this shall be my pleading,
That not with eyes unheeding
I have beheld the beauty
Of Earth and all things living.

ON THE MOOR

The life I left—to-day it seems
(So far remote) the stuff of dreams.

Wild nature here about me lies
Speechless and innocent and wise.

No question here, no argument,
No angered voice or discontent,

But only sound of winds that blew
In heaven when the earth was new,

And voice of waters downward hurled
Since the foundation of the world.

Have I awakened from the night
And found myself in spacious light?

Or lie I in the plane of dreams,
Held fast by that which only seems,

Soon to awake to human strife?
Which is the dream, and which the life?

FROM MOSCHUS

Ah me, ah me, the mallows in the garden,
    Or parsley green and the soft flower of dill,
        When their beauty dies,
    Live for another year and further birth.

But we, the men of might, when once we perish,
    Sleeping for very long, and very still,
        We the great and wise,
    Lie unawakened in the hollowed earth.

WORDS AND DEEDS

In what a little sum they disagree,
The more opponents talk, the less they see;
The more they work in fellowship, the more
They wonder why they stood apart before.

THE BELITTLER

By jot or by tittle
  I softly depress
The large to the little,
  The small to the less.

Though tightly they're tedded,
  Though close and thick
The strands are inthreaded,
  A hole I pick.

In character high and
  In luminous mind
A speck I espy and
  A blemish I find.

With total acquittal
  I cannot agree;
Be it ever so little,
  A flaw I see.

Glass houses are brittle—
  I leave them alone;
But somewhat I whittle
  From steel or stone.

A finger so lightly
  I lay on the spot,
You doubt if unsightly
  You think it or not.

Some fools, in their folly,
  To damage a name
Use broadside and volley
  And thunder and flame.

I who belittle
   Have ways of my own;
Glass houses are brittle,
   I cast not a stone.

NIDDERDALE

Of Eton, King's, and Magdalene
   No troubled thought can be,
And when delight attains its height
   I think of all the three.

And now upon this hillside,
   Sprawling in flowers and sun
I tie together three heads of heather
   And think of three as one;

And 'Eton, King's, and Magdalene',
   I spell for years to be,
'Love bind together, as I this heather,
   And hold in one the three'.

CONSECRATION

With lips alone MacAndrew sanctifies;
   A thing, it seems, is right because he's said it;
Still holier influence falls from Winkle's eyes;
   With him, a book is good because he's read it.

THE ROYAL HOTEL

Who will give me a prophylactic
Against that damnable dull Didactic,
Lecturing all and sundry there,
Occupying the central chair?
Into my ears I thrust my thumbs,
Still he beats upon the drums;
I fly, he comes through wall and door
And penetrates the upper floor;
Into my bed at last I creep
And seek escape in smothering sleep,
And through my dreams till break of day
I hear the dreary old donkey bray.

FOCUS

Life's littlenesses blur the instant scene,
And small and great are ill to judge between;
Time slowly brings the truth in focus. So
Men's portraits after death more like them grow.

FROM SOPHOCLES

Full many wonderful things there be,
  And none more marvellous is than Man.
He fareth over the foaming sea
  By storm and by hurricane,
And through the trough of towering waters travelleth he.

The deathless Earth untired, of gods
    Most old, he weareth down, when go
The ploughs at yearly periods
    And bend them to and fro;
And with the aid of the horse's brood he turneth the stiff
    clods.

Light-witted races of the air
    And nations of the field and sea
In coil of net and in woven snare
    He taketh captive—he
Most cunning, and trappeth whatsoever hath his lair

In wilds or walketh on the hill.
    With yoke on neck the shaggy steed
And mountain bull's untiring will
    He breaketh. He indeed
Of speech and airy thought himself hath found the skill,

And knoweth the springs of law's domain.
    Hard lodging hath he learned to fly
And stinging frost and smiting rain
    Under the open sky—
Resourceful ever. Nought encountereth he in vain

Of things to come. From Death alone
    No shelter shall his wit invent,
Albeit devisings of his own
    From the predicament
Of stubborn maladies a path of flight have shown.

This cunning, passing all his dreams in her inventiveness,
Man carrieth with him on his way, to hurt him or to bless.

OYΔEN MENEI

His hymn of change does Murphy sing,
Provoked by every rooted thing,
And never seems to feel, 't is strange,
The tedium of perpetual change.

SELF-EXPRESSION

'Myself', Alexis said, 'I must express',
And published nothing. He could do no less.

GENERALITIES

Of general statements said I know not who
'Each of them, even this one, is untrue'.

THE BRAINS TRUST

I

Said Satan, sniggering in his glee,
  'They've made an invention in London Town,
The neatest contrivance I ever did see
  For doing the sons of old Verity down.

O'er Britain's empire, and seas between,
  Through all the colonies and the dominions,
In a single moment this one machine
  Disseminates unconsidered opinions.

To him who invented it—Master sublime—
  I take off my shoes and I take off my hat;
I've fashioned some neat little things in my time,
  But never so simple an engine as that.'

II

Time was, the wise man thought before he spoke,
  And thus was deemed to be the true adviser;
But now the view is held by common folk
  That those who speak before they think are wiser.

POLITICS

Wherefore the art of politics
   (The noblest that should be)
Descends to low and sordid tricks,
   Is more than I can see.

But this I know, that gentlemen
   Have touched the fine machine
And soiled therein their hands, and then
   Have failed to wash them clean.

My son, be not as they; but fix
   Thy mind on high intent;
Open shall be thy politics,
   Nor false thy sacrament.

Guard thou thy troth. Who breaks a truce,
   Fair cause he may pretend,
But to himself, for all excuse,
   He shall not make amend.

For all his show and bravery,
   He goes down to the grave
Knowing himself at heart to be
   A traitor and a slave.

HOPELESS

Our Dismal Jemmy looks to-day
   Unusually dejected;
'Things seem to be', I heard him say,
   'Less bad than I expected.'

HISTORICUS

You say my evidence is brittle;
    You say, in fact, I fake it.
But history's written by the little;
    It is the great who make it.

YOREDALE

Here is a sound enthralling
Of waters ever falling,
Of waters falling and calling
    To woods and rocks unheeding;
Here, where the stream dark-breasted
Breaks over diamond-crested,
The voice is held arrested
    Of waters onward speeding.

What though the unresting river
Hastes forward? Here for ever
Stands still his voice that never
    A moment ceases sounding,
Nor e'er is drawn asunder
From woods and rocks whereunder
His monotone of thunder,
    As silence, hangs astounding.

BOMBINANS IN VACUO

A bee in your bonnet you've got;
   It's round it and in it and on it;
What worries you, Jock, if it's not
    A bee in your bonnet?

  It comes, and it goes, and anon it
Returns, and it rattles you, what?
   It's gone, and it's come, and it's gone; it

Has buzzed at your head till it's hot.
   I'll lay my last tizzy upon it—
You've got (and if not, I'll be shot)
    A bee in your bonnet.

Q

We took him from Oxford? Undoubtedly true.
From Oxford not seldom we've taken our queue.

MALVERN HILLS

I

Is this the rare
   And curious case
When limping Care
   Gives up the chase?
Or am I free
   Of sin and debt?
Or can it be
   That I forget?

II

Here, where I proudly lay me
   On open hill-top high,
No man may disobey me,
   For none is here but I.
I am the lord unchallenged,
   For, mark you, I shall brook,
Where none stand near to interfere,
   No rival voice or look.

On all things my impression
   I seal, and by my hand
My absolute possession
   I write of air and land,
Of heavily hung heavens,
   Of cloud-impurpled plain,
Nor is there heard a lifted word
   Disputing my domain.

My mind is no divider
   Of that which is its own;
I know no empire wider
   Than his who reigns alone;
Unshared is his dominion,
   And, whatsoe'er befall,
His Law and State are ultimate,
   Obeyed by one and all.

SOLITUDE

How fair, O Solitude, is thy face
  On sunny hillsides aflame with furze,
  Or where the green life in the woodland stirs.
There how winsome thou art, how full of grace,
How gentle and soft to kiss and to embrace.
  O then how stale and dusty and drear
  Men and their wearisome ways appear.

The sky clouds over, the air turns cold
  With angrier wind in the fading light,
  And rain monotonous drops, and comes the night.
How art thou fearful grown, how sour and old,
How clammy to handle, and eerie to behold.
  How warm they seem and desirable then,
  Friends and the welcoming ways of men.

FATHER CAMUS

In shade of rock and ashen glade
    From darkness into light
Cautious he comes, as half afraid,
    And shy of human sight;
His whispering rills collect and flow
    Together, and along they steal,
And under gardens green they go
    To turn a grumbling wheel;
Then out into the fields he makes
    His way by secret hedgerow cleft,
And gathers trickling streams and takes
    His tribute from the right and left.

And now large influence he brings
    From Wendy's pleasant plain
And Melburn Bury's garden springs
    And meadows filled with rain;
Under long Barrington he creeps,
    By bank and bush and cress concealed;
Among the trembling flowers he sleeps
    Of lovely Haslingfield;
Then mingles with the waters drawn
    From many an oozing Essex ridge,
And leads them from their saffron lawn
    To Grantchester and Grantabridge.

Now hushed and holy is his way
    In peaceful meadows green,
By hanging rose and willow grey,
    Sweet Poesy's demesne.
Lift up your heads, O Towers and Halls,
    Right royal be his archëd road,
As gliding under ancient walls
    He hallows Song's abode.

Lift up your heads: his waters flow
  In reverence as he stays his sight
On Paradise, and footing slow
  He passes, lingering with delight.

Then Magdalene bids him soft farewell,
  And sends him to the fen
Through banks asleep in asphodel
  Or loud with clamorous men.
He winds along from Ditton turn,
  And shadows in his sliding glass
Dark underleaf, or silver hern,
  Or azure wings that pass;
Then floods with Ouse at Ely's isle
  To swell the ranks of waters free
That spread their front of mile on mile
  To meet the legions of the sea.

SVI PRODIGVS

We constantly hear O'Flanagan say
  'I gave him a piece of my mind';
Which is why, when so much has been given away,
  So little remains behind.

THE EXCEPTION

Self-love and justice side by side
  Not often in one person dwell;
But loving self has Jorkins died,
  And just as well.

LEVELLING DOWN

If God had made all men equal,
  And fixed them firmly so,
  I'd like very much to know
What would have been the sequel.

No rivalry of endeavour?
  No splendid eminence?
  But only indifference
Everywhere and for ever?

Whoever had then competed
  In any race or game,
  All would have scored the same,
Solemnly undefeated.

When man is joining together
  What God has put asunder,
  It's likely that some may wonder,
Not without reason, whether

In spite of man's inventions
  Perhaps God was right.
  At least he possibly might
Have had the better intentions.

FLOS MALVAE

The cunning fashioner of things,
Mechanic, with unresting springs,
Marks on her dial the rathe and sere,
The morn and evening of the year.

The force that pushed the crocus up,
And lifted the great tulip cup,
Now lays across the numbered clock
The long hand of the hollyhock.

Behind his silent open face
Is heard, of Time, the measured pace,
Which keeps both dawn and afternoon
Aware of rhythm and ordered tune.

And whosoe'er essayed to sing
The scarlet and the gold of spring,
May set to rhyme at later hour
Fair linen of the mallow flower.

Printed in the United States
By Bookmasters